LAKE CHAMPLAIN FERRYBOATS

I.

— TO SEIZE CONTROL — THE CONFLICTS OVER LAKE CHAMPLAIN

(1609-1814)

A brief history by Jerry P. Williams

II.

TWO CENTURIES OF FERRY BOATING ON LAKE CHAMPLAIN

by Ralph Nading Hill

COVER PHOTOGRAPH:
BURLINGTON-PORT KENT FERRY M. V. CHAMPLAIN

Published by Lake Champlain Transportation Company,
Burlington, Vermont

i

Edited by Jerry P. Williams
Design by Battery Graphics
Map by Hamilton Greene
Printed by Queen City Printers Inc., Burlington, VT
Color Photographs by Jerry P. Williams

Lake Champlain Transportation Company thanks
Anthony Shaw for permission to republish
"Two Centuries of Ferryboating on Lake Champlain"
(copyright 1959, 1962, 1972), written by his uncle,
the late Ralph Nading Hill.
Also Meg Greene and Art Cohn for
their assistance with "To Seize Control—
The Conflicts over Lake Champlain"

FORWARD

Caniaderi Guarunte" was what the Iroquois Indians had named her: "the lake that is the gate to the country." After Lake Champlain's discovery in 1609, over two centuries of conflict would ensue before a young America would finally guarantee her safe future. Control of the lake during this period would be contested by the armies and navies of France, Great Britain, and the American colonists. Military control over this gateway between the heart of the colonies and Canada meant control over a large part of the northeast.

Once the sounds of cannonfire had ceased, Lake Champlain became a gateway for commerce. Visitors and residents appreciate the lake today as a prized resource cradled by the Adirondacks of New York and the Green Mountains of Vermont. But during the 17th, 18th, and three quarters of the 19th centuries, this lake provided the only practical means of transportation not only between the settlements along the Vermont and New York shores, but as a long and vital link in the through traffic between Montreal and the cities down the Hudson River to New York. Travelers seeking a direct route between these two cities—or points in between—made their way either on foot, horseback, or in stagecoaches over miles of rugged trails. Or they could relax in the comparative comfort of the vessels plying Lake Champlain between Whitehall, New York and St. Jean, Quebec. Local ferryboats also provided local travelers with a relatively comfortable and expedient link among the lakeshore ports.

Lake Champlain Ferryboats briefly traces the lake's historic role as a gateway for military conquest between 1609 and 1814. With peace the lake became a gateway for commerce focused on lumber, and mining operations. Ferryboating evolved, and this sixth largest lake in the country remains today one of the few with a busy fleet of ferries. Their lively story is presented here with a wealth of fascinating anecdotes reflecting the times as vividly as the boats and the men and women who ran them.

WILLIAM FADEN'S MAP SHOWING ARNOLD'S AMERICAN AND CARLETON'S
BRITISH FLEETS AT THE BATTLE OF VALCOUR ON OCTOBER 11, 1776.
Courtesy Lake Champlain Maritime Museum at Basin Harbor

iv

I.
—To Seize Control—
The Conflicts over Lake Champlain

(1609–1814)
A brief history by Jerry P. Williams

ake Champlain is a natural for ferryboats. The water-way flows north some 100 miles from Whitehall, New York to its confluence with the Richelieu River near the American-Canadian border. A long, narrow, north-south water highway, the lake has always created a need for getting from one side to the other and ferrying has been a part of the maritime lore of the region since prehistoric times. Native Americans, using birch-bark and dugout canoes, were certainly the first peoples to travel across the lake. Early European settlers developed the "bateau," a crude rowing vessel that was used to ferry military personnel and supplies throughout the region. Later came boats propelled by sailpower, horsepower, steam, and diesel.

For many years the development of ferries and ferry routes on Lake Champlain took a backseat to a continuing struggle for control of the strategic waterway. This struggle manifested itself during three distinct military contests for control of the lake in a period when water was the primary means of transportation. Each war had a naval component and naval squadrons proved critical to the outcome of the conflicts. Ferrying played a part in these military maneuvers, but it was during the periods of peace that settlement, commerce, and ferrying thrived.

Discovery of Lake Champlain

"The next day we entered the lake, which is of great extant, perhaps 50 or 60 leagues long. There I saw four beautiful islands . . . which formerly had been inhabited by savages. There are also several rivers which flow into the lake that are bordered by many fine trees, of the same sorts that we have in France. . . . Continuing our course in this lake on the west side I saw, as I was observing the country, some very high mountains on the east side, with snow on top of them [the Green Mountains]. . . . I saw on the south others not less high than the first, but they had no snow at all . . . ," stated Samuel de Champlain in describing the lake which eventually carried his name. In July of 1609, accompanied by a party of his Algonquin Indian guides, Champlain documented a water system which until then had been unknown to Europeans. But the exploration was halted by a confrontation with the Algonquin's traditional enemies, the Iroquois. With the help of Champlain's arquebus (an early type of firearm), the Iroquois, though greater in number, soon fled in terror. This important confrontation led to the formation of Indian and European alliances that would continue throughout the next 150 years of French and British conflict for domination of the Champlain Valley.

FRENCH AND INDIAN WARS

The Champlain Valley became one of the major theaters of conflict in a worldwide struggle between two of the great European powers—England and France. After building a series of temporary strongholds, the French built forts St. Frederick (1734) at Crown Point, and Carillon (1755) at Ticonderoga. Both were built at narrow parts of the lake and were France's way of staking claim to the rich Champlain Valley territory. In America, the last act of this long struggle was known as the French and Indian War and was staged largely in and around the Champlain Valley. The British mounted seasonal campaigns against the French in an attempt to drive them back out of the region. In 1758, a huge British army of 15,000 men under General James Abercrombie crossed Lake George in 900 bateaux and 100 whaleboats. In their poorly directed assault on a much smaller French force at Ticonderoga, the British lost an appalling 2,000 men in a single 24-hour period and were forced to retreat. In anticipation of another seasonal assault, the French constructed a fleet of warships to patrol the lake. As expected, in 1759 the British sent another large army under the leadership of General Jeffery Amherst, to drive the French from the valley. After routing the French from their forts, Amherst then built a naval squadron to capture control of the lake. The next year, the British were able to secure Canada from the French and the Champlain Valley found itself at peace—under the British flag.

THE AMERICAN REVOLUTION

For a brief period the Champlain Valley found itself in the midst of the more peaceful pursuits of land settlement and speculation. The calm, however, proved short-lived. On May 10, 1775, the lake became a major setting for a new conflict—the American Revolution. Colonel Benedict Arnold (commissioned by the State of Massachussetts), Vermont's own Ethan Allen, and 80 of his Green Mountain Boys captured Fort Ticonderoga (formerly Carillon) from the British. Gaining control of the strategically located fort proved a crucial early event in the Revolutionary War and galvanized the spirit of the colonials. In the fall and winter of 1775-76, flushed with the success of capturing the Champlain invasion route, the Americans decided to press their advantage and invade Canada. But this campaign proved a disaster, and by spring of 1776 the American army was in retreat back to Fort Ticonderoga. Meanwhile, the British army advanced as far south as St. John's, Quebec, but with the Americans as masters of the lake, were forced to delay their proposed takeover of the strategic waterway. Though in control of the lake the Americans still needed a navy to meet the pending British invasion from the north. The job of building this first American fleet fell to Benedict Arnold. Most of the new fleet was hewn from scratch in Skenesborough (Whitehall), New York beginning in the summer of 1776. Arnold's infant navy comprised fifteen vessels when it met Sir Guy Carleton's powerful British fleet off Valcour Island on October 11, 1776. Discovering too late the enormous advantage in the British fleet's firepower, Arnold resorted to a defensive battle plan, forcing the British to sail into the wind to engage him. The two squadrons exchanged firepower for five hours, with both sides sustaining heavy damage. By nightfall the Americans had expended three-fourths of their ammunition and lost their flagship, the schooner *Royal Savage* and the gunboat *Philadelphia*. Arnold and his officers managed a daring escape under the cover of darkness by rowing their battered vessels single file past the British blockade boats. The next morning, as the Americans attempted to reach the safety of Fort Ticonderoga, the British gave chase.

The result was a second battle on October 13, this one a running fight up the lake. Arnold, fighting aboard the galley *Congress*, and realizing he could not reach his lines, ordered five of his vessels into a small bay on the Vermont shore and intentionally set fire to them, denying them to the British. Now only four vessels remained in the American fleet and the British succeeded in taking control of the Lake Champlain invasion route. But it was October and the region was turning cold. The British command decided that they would delay their invasion southward until the spring of 1777 and the army moved back to Canada for the winter.

THE 1777 CAMPAIGN SAW A BRITISH ARMY UNDER THE COMMAND OF GENERAL JOHN Burgoyne advance through the lake without naval opposition. Their goal was to isolate New England by gaining control of Lake Champlain and the Hudson River. General George Washington, convinced the bulk of the British attack would be directed elsewhere, left Fort Ticonderoga and Mount Independence—both vital in blocking the British advance—seriously undermanned. Although outnumbered, the American troops under General Arthur St. Clair still appeared to have a chance at holding their crucial positions at both Fort Ticonderoga and Mount Independence. However, one critical oversight on the part of the Americans made the taking of these garrisons little more than a diversion for the British advance. Sugar Loaf Hill, dismissed by the American command as too steep to fortify, overlooked and was within cannon range of both Fort Ticonderoga and a portion of Mt. Independence. The British, seizing upon this oversight, dragged up their cannons and quickly fortified the hill. St. Clair, surprised by the strength of the British army, and with the threat of British guns aimed down on his troops, withdrew without a fight. His defeat was a terrible blow to the morale of the colonials. With St. Clair's defeat, King George III and his British troops believed the end of the American uprising was imminent. But Burgoyne's momentum was upset by a series of reversals; a significant one being the Battle of Bennington (August 17, 1777), where his defeat rekindled the spirit of the Americans. Burgoyne ultimately met a large and determined American force along the Hudson River at Saratoga. Here, the pride of the British army was tarnished as Burgoyne went down in defeat (October 17, 1777). Overall, this loss is considered a major turning point in the war.

Many historians point to the Lake Champlain naval campaign of 1776, crediting it with delaying the British advance for a year. This year gave the Americans precious time to better organize their army and meet Burgoyne at the critical moment. Had not Arnold and the Americans determined to hold Lake Champlain in 1776, the outcome of the Revolutionary War might have been much different.

Lake Champlain remained in British hands for the remainder of the war with farms and settlements around the lake essentially abandoned until the close of the conflict. With the war's end, the Champlain Valley experienced rapid resettlement and a need for all types of water transport. Small craft continued to be utilized and commercial lake sloops were built to handle the trade needs of the growing frontier region. Ferries powered by oar, sail, and horses appeared at many of the narrow lake crossings and by the end of the 18th and beginning of the 19th centuries, formal petitions for ferry rights were being placed before the Vermont and New York legislatures.

THE WAR OF 1812

But the sound of hostile cannon fire would echo once more on Lake Champlain. Britain, again at war with France, frowned upon any neutral power, especially a newly freed America, enjoying a trading relationship with her historic enemy. To prohibit further activity, the British resorted to seizure of American ships. America's reaction to this lack of respect for her neutrality led to the War of 1812.

Once again, a British naval fleet from Canada would utilize Lake Champlain as a stage for battle with America. Navy Lieutenant Thomas Macdonough was entrusted by the Secretary of the Navy: "to [never] suffer the enemy to gain the ascendancy on Lake Champlain." Macdonough, under President Madison's orders, was to build a fleet capable of turning the British ships back. He chose as a location for his hurried project Vergennes, Vermont, then an industrial town situated seven miles off Lake Champlain via the Otter Creek. The 734-ton brig *Saratoga* was built and launched only forty days after the wood of her hull was felled from the local forests. Another of his fleet, the *Ticonderoga*, was already under construction as a steamer for ferrying passengers when transformed into a sixteen gun schooner. In record time, Macdonough assembled a fleet that stood a fighting chance against the British force under Captain George Downie.

B. TANNER'S ENGRAVING OF A PAINTING BY HUGH REINAGLE DEPICTING
THE BATTLE OF PLATTSBURGH BAY, SEPTEMBER 11, 1814.
Courtesy Clinton County Historical Museum

The two fleets met at the Battle of Plattsburgh Bay on September 11, 1814. Early in the battle, Downie's *Confiance* seriously damaged Macdonough's *Saratoga*. However, in cleverly anchoring his vessels so that they might be rotated, Macdonough was able to bring fresh guns into the action. After more than two hours of intense cannon fire, the British surrendered their fleet, making Macdonough a national hero. The 10,000 British troops advancing near Plattsburgh under the command of Sir George Prevost, learned of the surrender and retreated to Canada.

The lake remained peaceful from then on. Lake Champlain now acted as a gateway for settlement and commerce instead of upheaval and war. The remainder of the century would see a tremendous growth in watercraft, canal building, and maritime activity as the lake reached its commercial zenith. Ferryboats were an integral part of this seascape and this brings us to their story.

COMMERCE ON LAKE CHAMPLAIN BLOSSOMED AFTER THE WAR OF 1812:
WHITEHALL, NEW YORK CIRCA 1816.
Courtesy Lake Champlain Maritime Museum at Basin Harbor

EARLY LAKE CHAMPLAIN TIMBER RAFT.
Courtesy Special Collections, University of Vermont Library

Steam Ferry.

24th April, 1830.

THE STEAM-BOAT

GEN. GREENE,

CAPTAIN DAN LYON,

WILL run until further notice in the following order, viz:

Leave Burlington at half past 8 o'clock in the morning, Sundays excepted, touching at Port Kent, and arrive at Plattsburgh at 12 o'clock.

Leave Plattsburgh at 2 o'clock P. M., and PORT KENT at 4 o'clock, and arrive at Burlington at half past 5 the same evening.

The following are the established rates of Ferriage

TO AND FROM PORT KENT.

Every four wheel pleasure Carriage on springs, drawn by two Horses, including driver,	\$2 00
Every two wheel pleasure Carriage on springs, drawn by one Horse, including driver,	1 50
Every Wagon or Sleigh drawn by two Horses, including driver,	1 50
Every Wagon, Cart or Sleigh drawn by one Horse, including driver,	1 25
Every Cart drawn by two Oxen, including driver	1 50
Every additional person, Horse or Ox,	50
Every foot passenger, (children under 12 years of age, half price,)	50
Cattle in droves, each	25
Sheep and Hogs in droves, each	6
Parties of pleasure going and returning the same day, not less than 12 persons, each	25

A reasonable sum will be added to the above prices to and from Plattsburgh.

The above rates will be charged, until the first day of November, after which time the company reserve to themselves the right of charging those rates of ferriage which are established and allowed by law.

Steamer General Greene 75 ft. Built at Shelburne Harbor, Vermont.
1830 Poster of the Champlain Ferry Company.

II.
Two Centuries
of Ferryboating on Lake Champlain

by Ralph Nading Hill

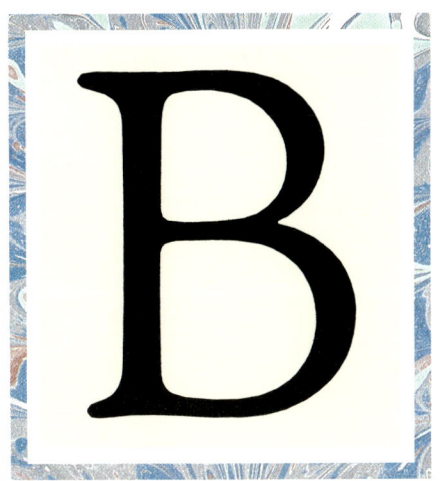

ECAUSE THE FIRST ATTEMPTS WERE BY TRIAL AND ERROR AND service was often intermittent, the dates when the first regular ferries ran at the lake's major crossings are hard to establish with authority. Some that were given state charters never ran and some ran that never had charters. In 1785 a man named McKenzie established a ferry from Moriah to the Vermont shore. The only written testimony, curiously enough, that Allen Wood, presumably the first ferryman between Orwell and Montcalm Landing, was operating a boat in 1802 consists of his name and date carved on a flat rock on the Vermont side. Just as elusive are the names of some of the landings. Although Larrabee's Point has been known by that name since John Larrabee arrived in 1783, it was previously called Shaw's Landing and a ferry was then running to Ticonderoga. There were, to muddy the water further, other ferries running abreast of this one—from Smith's Landing and Blood's Point to Montcalm Landing, directly below Mount Defiance on the west shore. But Montcalm Landing, as the line steamboat and railroad terminal has been called for generations, was previously known as Port Marshall!

With the evidence available it is safe to state that the crossings (proceeding north) from Chipman Point to Wright's, Orwell to Montcalm Landing, Larrabee's Point to Ticonderoga, Chimney Point to Crown Point and Port Henry, Arnold's Bay to Bessboro (Westport), Basin Harbor to Rock Harbor, Kingsland Bay to Grog Harbor and Charlotte to Essex were all established before the close of the 18th century. Whether two other abandoned crossings in the extreme south, Benson to Putnam and Cold Springs to Dresden, were active in the very early days is unknown.

The land north of Burlington was a forested buffer first between the British in the south and the French in the north, and later, during the Revolution, between the British in Canada and the Americans to the south. Thus some of the ferries in the Champlain Islands did not operate regularly until shortly after the beginning of the 19th century.

The ingenuity of early freshwater boatmen found expression in a curious variety of craft. Some were merely floats of cedar logs pinned to stringers with a railing containing rowlocks on each side. Long primitive oars, setting poles which could be thrust against the bottom in shallow places, and sweeps laboriously eddying the water in the stern afforded adequate if creeping transport for teams or loads of cattle. The float became in turn an oar-propelled, then sail-driven scow with the sail often on one side to afford cargo space amidships and with lee boards to help keep the freight on its feet. "The sail-rigged scow boat with us is institutionalized," announced an observer in the northern islands. And so it was on some crossings throughout the 19th and even during the early years of the 20th century.

"Now nothing but the humble ferryboat . . . was seen," wrote Carolyn Royce. "Barber at the Point, and Ring at Rock Harbor saw each others' sails swing and fill in the same wind, or flap idly against the mast in a maddening calm. Further down the lake another sail, that of McNeil, ferrying from Charlotte to Essex, might be discerned. . . ."

SAIL POWERED FERRY AT LARRABEE'S POINT CROSSING.
Courtesy Special Collections, University of Vermont Library

Benjamin Bell, whose schooner was the first ferry from Grand Isle to Cumberland Head, charged 83 cents for man and horse, but 38 cents for a single man and 46 cents for a single horse. History does not divulge the reason for the extra cent for a horse presumably other than the man's own mount. Cows crossed for 38 cents and hogs and calves for 8.

The *Lion*, as Bell called his craft, suffered a peculiar accident in 1813. While crossing to Cumberland Head she was fired upon and besieged by three British row galleys which had been lying under cover at Point-Au-Roche. The British released the crew but ran the *Lion* ashore and set her afire. A later appraisal revealed that she was still sound. In the best tradition of Yankee defiance and frugality Bell rebuilt her and returned her to ferry duty.

In 1788 "Admiral" Gideon King built in Burlington two cutters for service to Essex and Plattsburgh. From 1790 to 1800 eight 30-ton sloops were built at Burlington alone. At least one of these, the *Lady Washington*, carried contraband, for she was fitted up with false bulkheads. Prior to 1815 twenty-two additional sloops, several weighing 75 tons, were launched in Burlington Bay and other ports. Many of the best early builders, like Daniel Wilcox and Benjamin Boardman, had brought their skills with them from southern New England.

An event of importance to a business chained to the vagaries of the wind was the filing in Washington, in 1819, of a patent to Mr. B. Langdon of Whitehall for a horse-powered ferry. Boatmen on the lake and on the Hudson to the south readily adopted Mr. Langdon's invention which at first seemed a hardship on the horses, according to a traveler in 1820, "but this is an illusion as it seems very immaterial to their comfort whether they advance with their load or cause the basis on which they labour to recede."

"The ferryboat," the passenger declared, "is of the most singular construction. A platform covers a wide, flat boat. Underneath the platform there is a large horizontal solid wheel which extends to the sides of the boat, and there the platform or deck is cut through and removed so as to afford sufficient room for two horses to stand on the flat surface of the wheel, one horse on each side, and parallel to the gunwale of the boat. The horses are harnessed in the

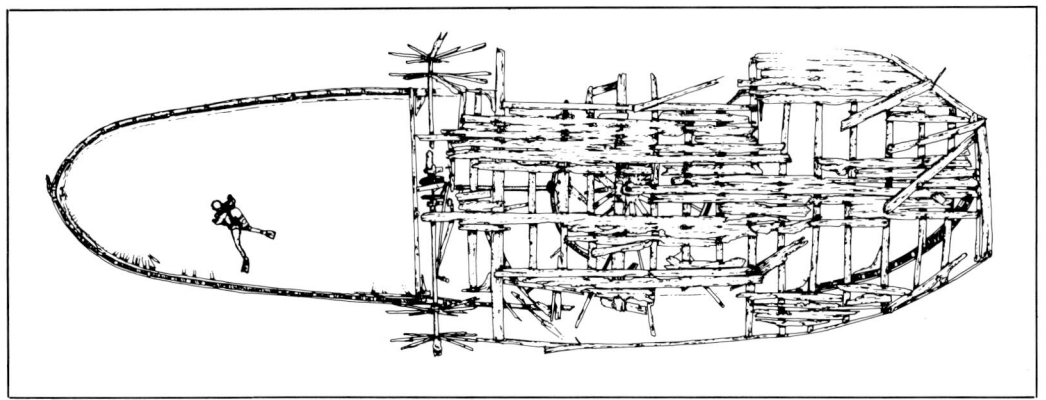

THE WRECK OF A HORSE FERRY IN BURLINGTON BAY. THE LARGE,
HORIZONTAL WHEEL THAT PROPELLED THE SIDEWHEELS IS VISIBLE
BENEATH THE FRAGMENTED DECKING. PHOTOMOSAIC BY SCOTT HILL,
MILTON SHARES, AND DENNIS FLOSS.
Courtesy Vermont Division for Historic Preservation.

usual manner for teams, the whiffletrees being attached to stout iron bars fixed horizontally at a proper height into posts, which are a part of the fixed portion of the boat. The horses look in opposite directions, one to the bow and the other to the stern; their feet take hold of channels or grooves cut in the wheels in the direction of radii; they press forward and, although they advance not, any more than a squirrel in a revolving cage or than a spit dog at his work, their feet cause the horizontal wheel to revolve in a direction opposite to that of their own apparent motion. This, by a connection of cogs, moves two vertical wheels, one on each wing of the boat. . . . The horses are covered by a roof furnished with curtains to protect them in bad weather and do not appear to labour harder than common draft horses with a heavy load."

The "superior Horse-Boat *Eagle*," probably of this type, was running three trips a day between Basin Harbor and Westport in 1841. Six horses drove another between Charlotte and Essex between 1821 and 1827, but this was of a different design since three horses, yoked together on each side of the deck, transmitted their power directly to the wheels through treadmills. This was the arrangement employed on the *Gypsy* which Asahel Barnes of Chimney Point ran to Port Henry for a few years before the Civil War. As contrasted with the Langdon method where the horizontal wheel trod by the horses was geared directly to both paddle wheels, the treadmills provided uncertain navigation, for if the horses on the left treadmill walked faster than those on the right the ferry was bound to veer sharply to starboard regardless of what the helmsman might do. The magic ingredient of a straight true course was the long whip of the "engineer" who sat usually in one of the passenger's buggies and applied encouragement to one team or another, depending on which was lagging. Mr. Barnes all but overcame this difficulty by importing some even-gaited Canadian ponies.

The motive power that blew the lid off the world of transportation was, of course, steam. Champlain was the first lake in the world to boast a regularly scheduled steamboat. Launched less than a year after Fulton's triumphant voyage to Albany on the *Clermont*, the paddleboat *Vermont* entered service in the spring of 1809, to be followed in the course of ten decades by twenty-eight similar vessels, the last built in 1906. They have received due attention and are considered here only insofar as they served as ferries. Many of them steamed strictly on "line run," the length of the lake from St. Johns to Whitehall, as links with the Hudson River boats in a kind of early inland water thruway between New York and Montreal. When railroads on both sides of the lake replaced them and they ceased to be indispensable carriers on this heavily traveled route their schedules were integrated with those of the trains to provide, with the boats of Lake George and the Hudson River until 1932, what was advertised as the finest summer excursion in America. Boating on Lake Champlain is a vast subject, as may readily be appreciated by the registrations of 1868 when 600 vessels of all kinds: steamers, canal boats, schooners, sloops and tugs, were entered upon the rolls. Their aggregate tonnage was about 40,000.

Steam ferries did not at first supplant those driven by wind or horses. The *Vermont*, like the *Clermont*, was clumsy. It did not tie up at way-landings but anchored offshore and disgorged its passengers over the side in small boats. In the early years there was no steamboat wharf in Plattsburgh harbor. Passengers from the line boats disembarked off Ransom's Landing at Cumberland Head where, with ferry passengers from Grand Isle, they were sailed around the point to Plattsburgh in pirogues or piraguas. These narrow, long, flat-bottomed vessels with lee boards were very common on more sheltered American waterways during the early 19th century. Carrying high narrow-headed sails, their two unsupported masts bent like marsh grass in the wind.

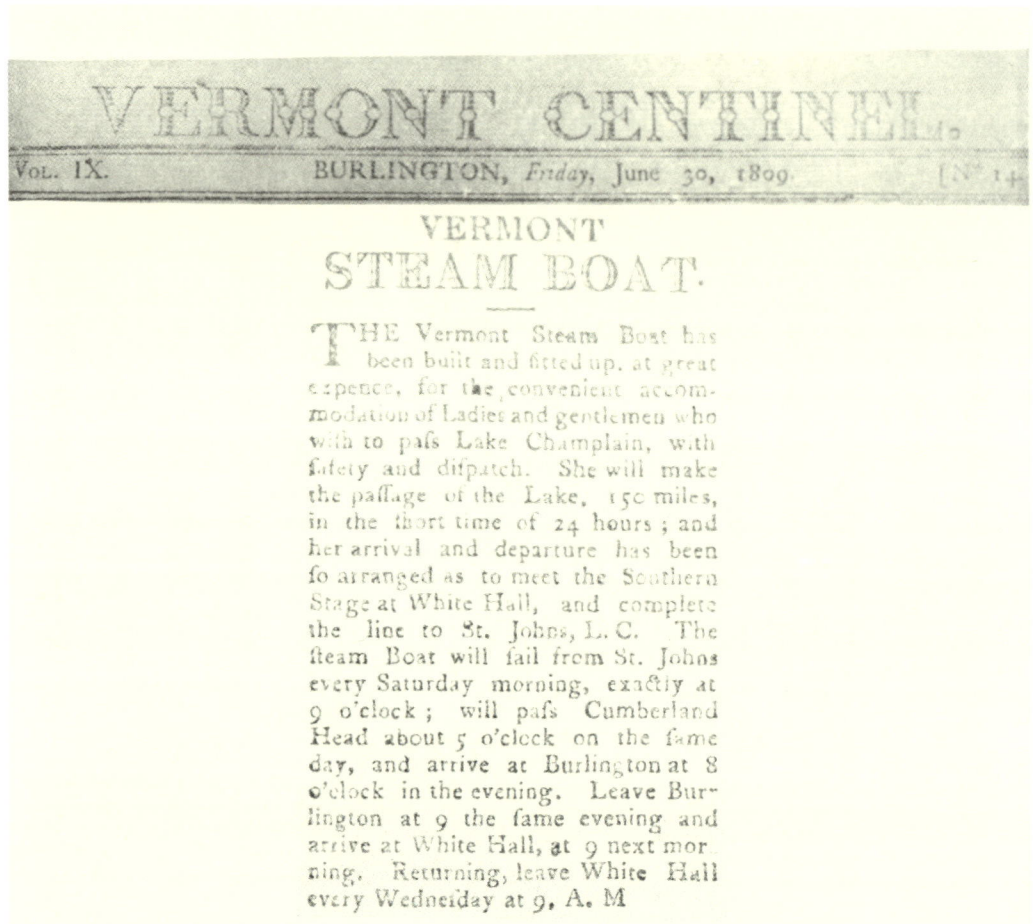

THE *Vermont* HAD THE HONOR OF BEING THE SECOND STEAMBOAT TO BE REGULARLY OPERATED IN COMMERCIAL SERVICE ANYWHERE IN THE WORLD.

Tall funnels exhaling clouds of smoke from hissing wood-burning boilers were first to be seen on the longer ferry runs. In 1825 the Champlain Ferry Company placed the 75-foot, 8-mile-an-hour *General Greene* in service between Burlington and Port Kent. A one-way crossing cost $2.00 for a "four-wheel pleasure carriage on springs, drawn by two horses, including the driver," and 50 cents less for a two-horse wagon or sleigh or a two-ox cart. The fare for a single ox, horse or person was 50 cents, while "parties of pleasure going and returning the same day" crossed at half price. For his monthly salary of $25.00 the captain operated the boat, collected fares and freight charges, and boarded his crew of six at $1.67½ cents a week. At the end of eight years of shuttle service the *General Greene* was replaced by the larger *Winooski* on this run.

Other early steamers on ferry routes exclusively were the *Macdonough*, which inaugurated regular service between St. Albans and Plattsburgh in 1825, and the *Water Witch*, whose route was Vergennes to Whitehall from 1832 to 1836. When steam proved too expensive on the short Charlotte-Essex crossing the Messrs. McNeil and Ross entered their new steamer *Washington* on the hotly contested north-south line run while McNeil's ferry horses victoriously

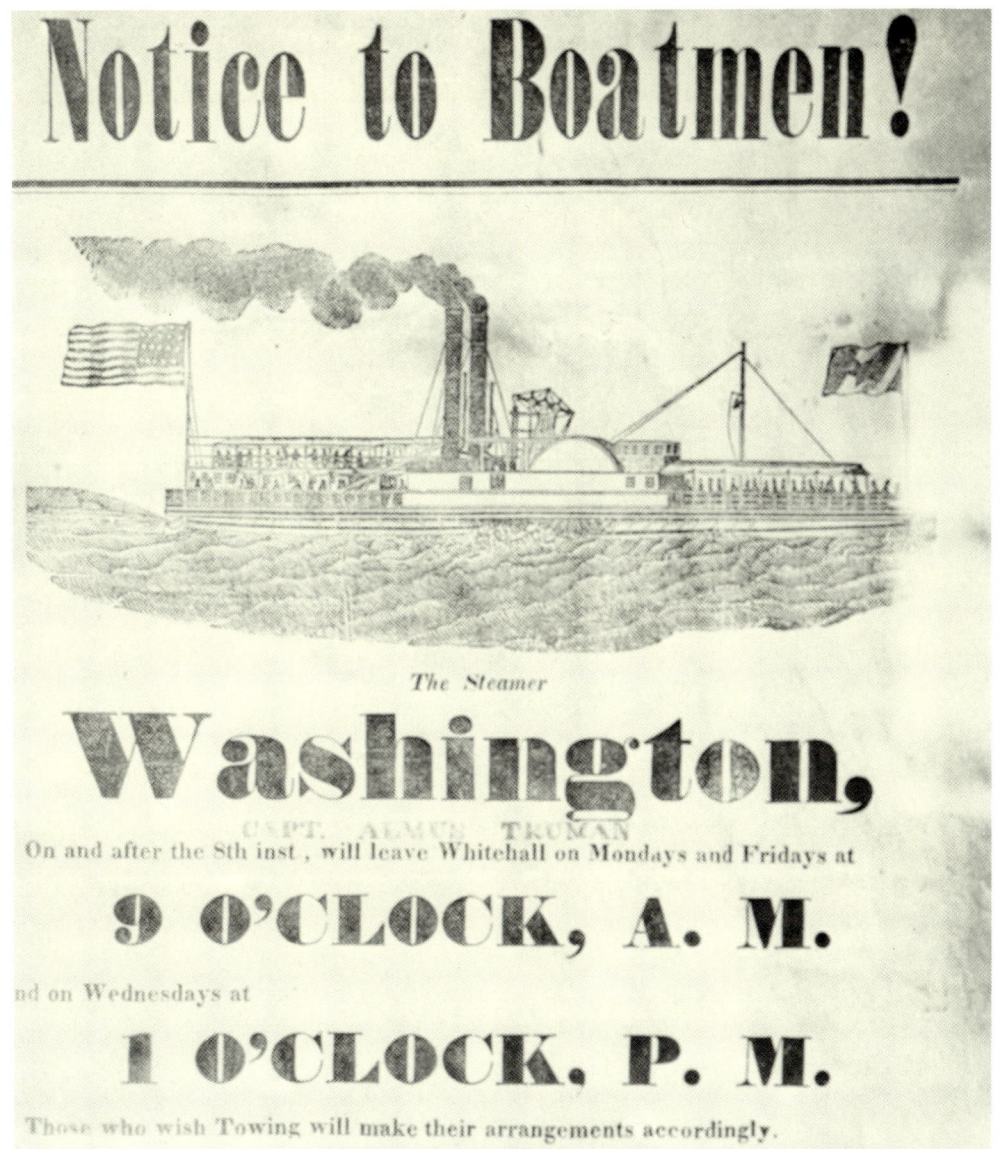

STEAMER *Washington*
POSTER OF THE CHAMPLAIN TRANSPORTATION COMPANY, CIRCA 1840

returned to their treadmills. These and other steamers, together with the companies that ran them, were all engulfed by the Champlain Transportation Company which in 1825 established headquarters in Burlington and has remained there ever since.

Nothing that happened on the Hudson River in the stock-watering, hijacking mid-19th century was without its counterpart on Lake Champlain, except that the local Drews, Fisks and Vanderbilts operated on a smaller scale. The methods used by the directors of the Transportation Company to dominate the north-south raceway and the most lucrative ferry route are a primer in monopoly. They would first try and usually succeed in buying out their competitors. Failing in this they would start a rate war and starve them out. In the case of the *Francis Saltus* they resorted to piracy. The *Saltus* was built in Whitehall in 1844 as a through-service opposition boat. Its owners did not capitulate until the Transportation Company in desperation produced the 240-foot *United States* with its superior speed of nineteen miles an hour.

In 1852 the monopoly strangely decided to sell all its boats including the recently acquired *Saltus* to the Rutland and Burlington Railroad. There were then no tracks through the Vermont islands to Montreal and the Rutland at Burlington needed a connection on the west side of the lake with the Grand Trunk Railroad at Rouses Point. The Rutland, as the directors of the Transportation Company had undoubtedly calculated, did not have much luck in the steamboat business. After two years it was forced to return the boats at a painful sacrifice. But the *Francis Saltus* was not included in the deal. The Rutland had meanwhile sold her to the Plattsburgh and Montreal Railroad which had just opened its line from the Canadian border to Plattsburgh and needed a ferry connection with the railroads at Burlington (for there were then no tracks south of Plattsburgh on the west side of the lake).

T HE *Saltus* THUS ENTERED A NEW ROLE AS AN OPPOSITION FERRY AND ONCE AGAIN APPEARED in competition with her former owners, the Champlain Transportation Company. The complicated machinations that followed amounted to an offer to representatives of the Plattsburgh and Montreal that if they would lay up the *Saltus* and allow the Transportation Company to ferry the railroad's passengers to Burlington on its own boat, the *United States*, the monopoly would make it worth the railroad's while. Accordingly in the spring of 1856 the *Saltus* was laid up in Plattsburgh and for a time all was serene.

But the Transportation Company could not abide the thought of the *Saltus* ready under the slightest pretext to spring forth again. On June 18 one of its officers, Captain Lot Chamberlain, took a crew to Plattsburgh, boarded the *Saltus*, put the watchman ashore, got up steam and sailed the *Saltus* out of enemy waters. Eventually, after hot litigation, the courts returned her to her rightful owners. But the monopoly was not to be dissuaded by the edicts

CHARLES DICKENS WROTE IN 1842 " . . . THE *Burlington* IS A PERFECTLY EXQUISITE ACHIEVEMENT OF NEATNESS, ELEGANCE AND ORDER. THE DECKS ARE DRAWING ROOMS; THE CABINS BOUDOIRS, CHOICELY FURNISHED AND ADORNED WITH PRINTS, PICTURES, AND MUSICAL INSTRUMENTS; EVERY NOOK AND CORNER OF THE VESSEL IS A PERFECT CURIOSITY OF GRACEFUL COMFORT AND BEAUTIFUL CONTRIVANCE . . . "

of a judge. Later, while the *Saltus* was docked at St. Johns, Captain Chamberlain again seized her on a technicality (upheld by the Supreme Court of Montreal), steamed her across the border to the Company's shipyard at Shelburne Harbor, tied her up, then removed and hid part of her machinery.

The immortal climax of this series of events was described in later years by Captain Robert White:

> "One memorable Sunday about one hundred men came from Plattsburgh on the sloop *Hercules* for the purpose of taking the *Saltus* back, by force if necessary. The C.T.Co. was, however, prepared, having the steamers *United States* and *Canada* there with their crews and having also dismantled the engine of the *Saltus*. . . . I saw Sheriff Flanagan draw a revolver on Judge Smalley but the Judge did not scare a bit. . . . The C.T.Co. finally moved the *Saltus* inside the wreck, ran a chain cable ashore and around a tree, and Henry Campbell sat on the chain, a revolver in his hand, and dared anyone to remove the cable."

The fight moved again to the courts with the result that the monopoly had to purchase the *Saltus* again and pay costs and damages. After that it took no more chances and scuttled her once and for all.

The only difference between the line paddleboats and those built for ferry duty was that the former were larger and, with their cabins, more luxurious. Regardless of their length and weight they all drew less than ten feet of water and were thus admirably suited for service anywhere on the lake, whether in the narrow channel leading to Whitehall or in shallow ferry and way landings. The 166-foot *Saranac*, built in Shelburne Harbor in 1842, was specifically designed for the Burlington-Port Kent run although for a time she was involved on line service in the war with the *Saltus*. Later Plattsburgh and St. Albans were added to her Burlington-Port Kent schedule.

Many of these vessels were very fast even by present-day standards. In 1852 the polished engine of the 250-foot *R. W. Sherman* (later called the *America*) drove her from Port Kent to Burlington in exactly 27 minutes at the rate of twenty knots. This record stands to the present day. One reason for the *Sherman's* speed was her narrow hull—too narrow, in fact, for optimum stability. The Company widened her four feet near the water line and she never again

STATION HOUSE, HOTEL AND STEAMBOAT LANDING, AT ROUSE'S POINT, NEW YORK.

Courtesy Special Collections, University of Vermont Library

attained her former speed.

The coming of the railroads had, as we have seen, added to the ferries a new and indispensable role as train connections. Prior to the building of the short line south to Plattsburgh, the bustling railroad and steamboat terminal of the north was Rouses Point. There passengers for New York and Boston took the line boats to Whitehall or the railroad ferry to Burlington to make connections with the Vermont Central or the Rutland and Burlington.

Probably the most unusual of all the lake's ferries was the 258-foot *Oakes Ames*, built in Marks Bay south of Burlington (Oakledge) almost directly opposite the Transportation Company's shipyard at Shelburne Point. The Marks Bay shipyard with its carpenter and blacksmith shops, stocks and ways has vanished without a trace, and it is hard to visualize the animated scene there in 1868 when the 1,145-ton steamer slid into the small bay. The *Oakes Ames* had railroad tracks across her lower deck which enabled her to ship a small train across the lake. Captain N.B. Proctor, her designer, builder and first master, designed also a "self-adjusting railroad bridge" which, with the help of an engine on shore, could quickly transfer loaded cars from the shore to the boat. With two engines, one for each sidewheel, the *Ames* could turn around within her own length and travel at least nineteen miles an hour.

The northern terminal for trains and boats having moved south from Rouses Point to Plattsburgh, the *Ames* served as a traveling railroad bridge between the Plattsburgh and Montreal and the Rutland and Burlington railroads, saving eighteen miles over the shortest rail

13

WRECK OF STEAMER *Champlain* AT STEAM MILL POINT NEAR
WESTPORT, NEW YORK, JULY 16, 1875.
Courtesy Special Collections, University of Vermont Library

route between Boston and Montreal and nearly thirty between Ogdensburg and Boston. She made four daily trips in each direction. The Champlain Transportation Company acquired her, inevitably, and made her over into a luxurious line boat, but she served in this role only a year and a half, for on a quiet summer night in 1875 her pilot miscalculated and ran her full speed onto Steam Mill Point near Westport. Although no lives were lost, the *Champlain*, as she was now called, was a total wreck.

IN THE MID-19TH CENTURY IMMIGRANTS FROM CANADA POURED THROUGH THE SLUICE OF the Champlain Valley into the cities of the east. For several decades a cavalcade of Irish, ascending the St. Lawrence to disembark at Montreal, steamed south on the line steamboats from Rouses Point to Plattsburgh. A babble of brogue echoed in the lake ports and the ferries, loaded with motley belongings, resembled battlefields after the din of war had passed.

As early as 1827 Captain Basil Hall of the Royal Navy described a crowded Lake Champlain steamboat bulging with tourists, businessmen and Irish immigrants, one of whom, sitting apart from the others on a bundle containing her scanty store of worldly goods and gear tied up in a threadbare handkerchief, reminded him of a painting by Raphael. The sight of Irish "in infinite tribes overflowing by every outlet to the States" intrigued Nathaniel Hawthorne in Burlington. He described the men as exhibiting "lazy strength and careless merriment and the women" with far plumper waists and bonnier limbs as well as bolder faces, than our shy and slender females." The ferryboats had deposited at the wharves a potpourri of merchants from Montreal, British officers from volunteer garrisons, French Canadians, Scotsmen of a better class, gentlemen of the South on a pleasure tour, country squires on business, the wandering Irish and of course great numbers of Yankees with horse wagons and ox teams.

The lake ports were junctions of immigration south from Canada and of westward migrating New Englanders. The latter movement had begun in earnest after the War of 1812 and was greatly augmented in 1823 with the opening of the Champlain Canal to the Hudson River. Every Tuesday and Saturday during the 1830s and 40s, canal packets left Vergennes, seven miles up the Otter Creek, for Whitehall, the Hudson River, the Erie Canal and points west. For a time there was, as had been said, a steam ferry between Vergennes and Whitehall; others carried hopeful ex-farmers and their families in bulging wagons from Vergennes to Westport or Port Henry on the first lap of their trek towards the sunset.

Such was the traffic that ferry proprietors built inns at their landings—at McNeil's in Charlotte, at Chimney and Chipman points, at Cold Springs and at Wright's. Returning to New England from Niagara, Hawthorne admired the Greek Revival hotel, subsequently destroyed by fire, on the shore at Larabee's Point:

"On the banks of the lake, within ten yards of the water, stood a pretty white tavern with a piazza along its front. A wharf and one or two stores were close at hand and appeared to have a good run of trade, foreign as well as domestic; the latter with Vermont farmers and the former with vessels plying between Whitehall and British Dominions. Altogether this was a pleasant and lively spot. I delighted in it, among other reasons, on account of the continual succession of travelers who spent an idle quarter of an hour in waiting for the ferryboat: affording me just enough time to make their acquaintance, penetrate their mysteries, and be rid of them without the risk of tediousness on either side."

Indeed to learn how people lived and what they owned, whether animal or vegetable, it was not necessary to observe the kitchens or barnyards of the hinterlands for they yielded their contents to the decks of the ferries.

Vermont II BUILT 1871—IN COST, SIZE, DISPLACEMENT AND HORSEPOWER,
THE *Vermont II* WAS WITHOUT PEER ON THE LAKE.
Courtesy Special Collections, University of Vermont Library

For the ferries, for the line steamers, for the iron-laden barges of Port Henry, for the skippers of lumber tows in Burlington, for the masters of sloop-rigged canal boats and pinflats alike, the last years of the 19th century were years of unbridled prosperity. They were also drowsy years of the veranda vacation, of cool summers and green watering places.

"Leaving Burlington by the morning boat, the party will find carriages in attendance at Port Kent (or they may transport their own by the steamer) to convey them to both places, and after a day of exciting enjoyment, may return to Burlington by the evening steamer. After viewing the stupendous operations of nature at the Chasm, they may expatiate among the trees in the pleasure of a picnic, or an excellent meal will be found at the 'Chasm House' nearby."

At Cliff Haven carriages with coachmen in costly livery met the Burlington boats and whisked passengers to towering Hotel Champlain on the ridge at Bluff Point. The grandeur of the hotel, frequently the summer White House during the administration of President McKinley, was rivaled by that of the steamer *Vermont II* with her stateroom hall of walnut, chestnut and gilt 175 feet long, with 61 staterooms, president's and bridal rooms, and a dining room for 150 persons. She carried a crew of sixty.

Having begun its reign eleven years before that of the queen whose name the era adopted, the Transportation Company by the opening of the 20th century had, like Her Majesty, grown plump, stately and somewhat arthritic, with a built-in sense of manifest destiny. Not long after the end of the first World War, however, the directors began to suspect that the old era was not going to last forever, that the horseless carriage was more than an experiment, and that it was not enough to advertise the line as "The Oldest Steamboat Company in the World."

Evans-Wadhams-Wolcott & Plattsburgh PASSING IN THE ICE CHANNEL AT
THE GRAND ISLE FERRY CROSSING

Valcour LIFEBOAT FRAMING *Adirondack* ON THE BURLINGTON, VERMONT –
PORT KENT, NEW YORK FERRY CROSSING.

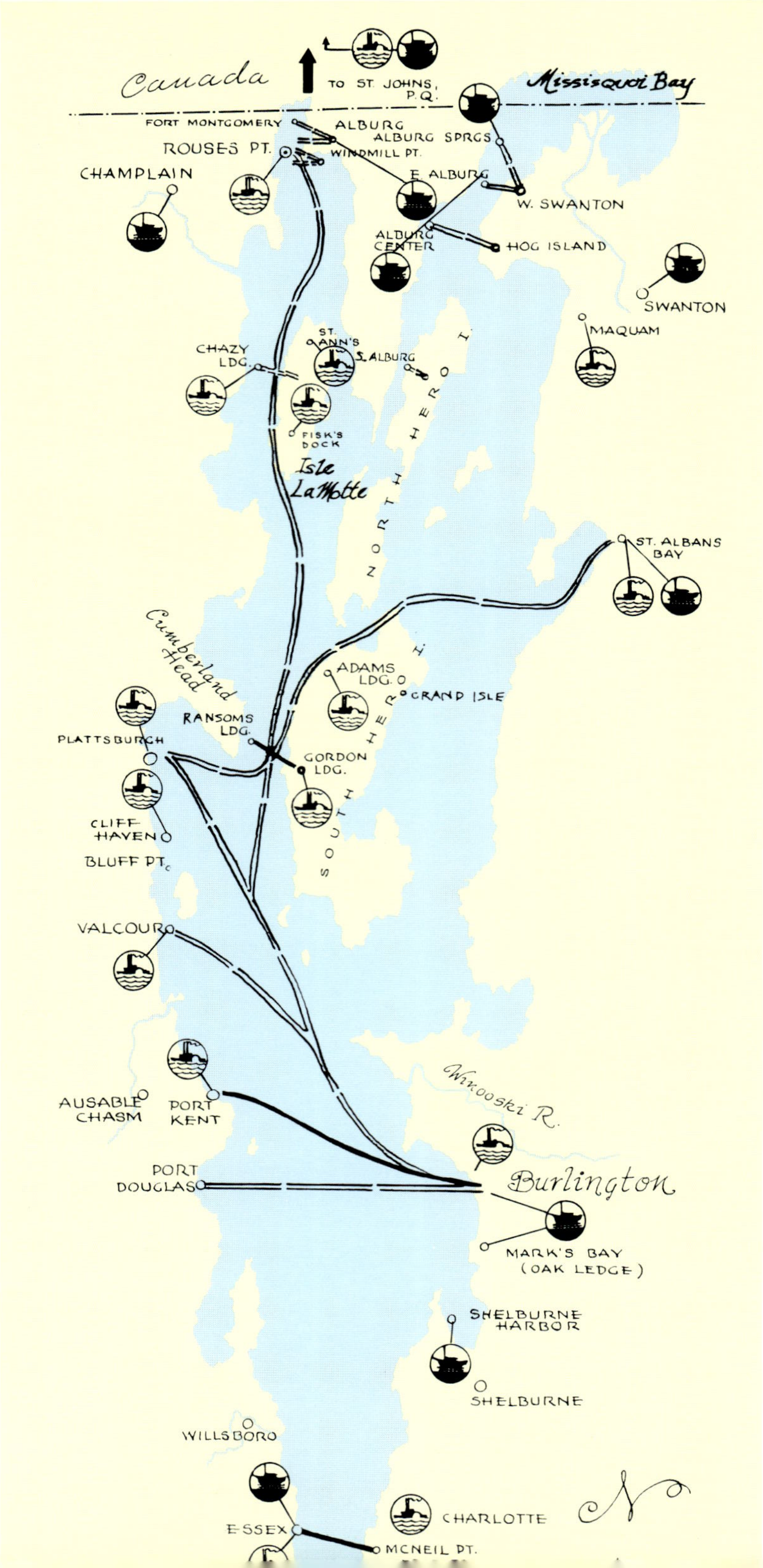

Legend

— ACTIVE FERRY CROSSINGS
== ABANDONED FERRY CROSSINGS
🚢 OLD SHIPYARDS
🏛 MAIN STEAMBOAT LANDINGS

ECOLE CHAMPLAIN
KINGSLAND BAY
FORT CASSIN
VERGENNES
OTTER CREEK
ROCK HARBOR
KIMBALL'S LDG.
BASIN HARBOR
ADAMS LDG.
ARNOLD'S (FERRIS) BAY
BARBERS PT.
WESTPORT (BESSBORO)
CROG HARBOR
CHIMNEY PT.
PORT HENRY
FORT ST FREDERIC
PUTT'S PT.
W. BRIDPORT
STONE'S FERRY LDG.
CROWN PT.
FIVE MILE PT.
STONY PT.
WATCH PT (CATTLE FERRY)
KERBY PT.
(SHAW LDG.)
LARRABEES PT.
BEADLE'S COVE
TICONDEROGA FORT.
MT INDEPENDENCE
MECURE'S
ORWELL
MONTCALM LDG. (PORT MARSHALL)
CHIPMAN PT.
WRIGHTS
PUTNAM STA.
O STONY PT.
BENSON LANDING
POULTNEY R.
Lake George
DRESDEN STA.
COLD SPRINGS
WHITEHALL (SKENESBORO)

BURLINGTON, VERMONT-PORT KENT, NEW YORK FERRY *Valcour* WITH
VERMONT'S MT. MANSFIELD IN BACKGROUND

MAIN ENGINE OF THE *Champlain* BEING TENDED BY THE OILER

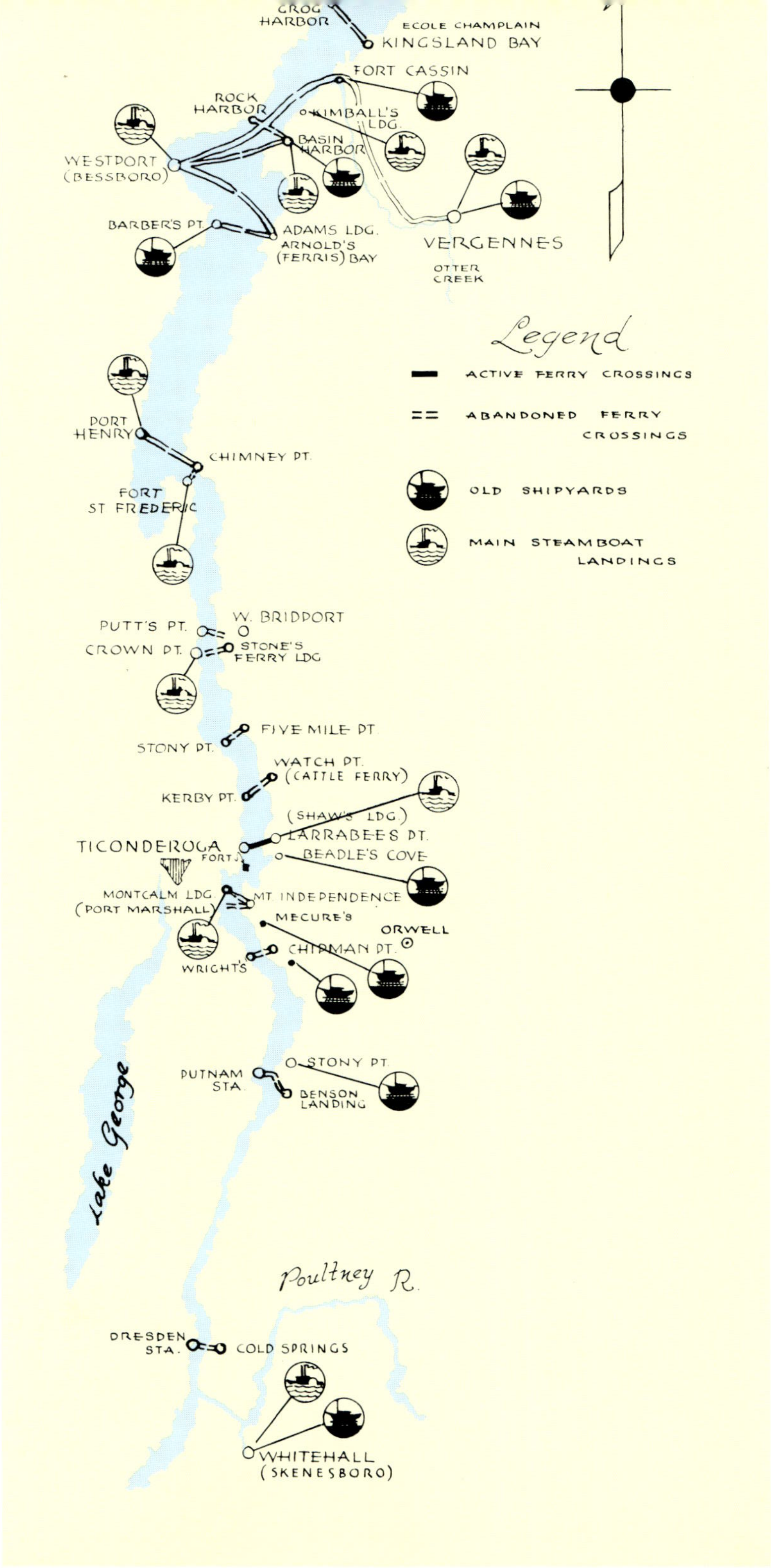

17

Before

Chateaugay—THE FIRST STEEL-HULLED STEAMER ON LAKE CHAMPLAIN—
BEFORE AND AFTER CONVERSION TO AN AUTO FERRY IN 1925.
Courtesy Special Collections, University of Vermont Library.

After

A NEW GENERATION OF TRAVELERS WEARING GOGGLES AND CLUTCHING BLUE BOOKS WAS raising dust along the roads to the ferry landings. Clearly steam and gasoline had to mix. In 1925 the iron-hulled *Chateaugay*, laid up for several years at Shelburne Harbor for want of business, was shorn of part of her stateroom hall and cabins fore and aft to make room for cars. The *Ticonderoga* abandoned the Westport-St. Albans run to join the *Chateaugay* on the shuttle between Burlington and Port Kent.

Older travelers will recall driving over the perilously narrow gangplanks of the *Ticonderoga*, having the air let out of their tires or deckhands stand on the running boards so that their high-bodied vehicles would not strike the ceiling of the forward promenade deck; having the gas temporarily drained out of their tanks and their cars jockeyed about between the stanchions and backed up as far as the paddleshaft on either side of the engine room. In the course

18

of her daily run to the train connection at Montcalm Landing even the proud *Vermont III*, famished for through-passengers, took on cars at Plattsburgh and Burlington.

There were a few days of glory for one of the steamers during the flood of 1927 when Vermont rivers wrought almost total havoc on railroad and highway bridges. The *Chateaugay* was the only link between northern Vermont and New York. For two weeks her boilers were never given a chance to cool as she plowed through swollen waters mined with floating trees, barns and dead cows. Loaded to the guards with beef, cement, lumber, mail and Red Cross supplies, she had no room, according to Captain John Montgomery, "to put a chicken on her anywhere."

The Transportation Company had enjoyed so many decades without competition that when independent operations started running car-carrying ferries virtually abreast of the large steamers, the old line scarcely knew what to do about them. The first of the new interlopers was Captain Elisha N. Goodsell, a resourceful Yankee who had cut his teeth in the ferry business in the Islands. His family had had experience competing even with themselves. In 1882 Goodsell's father put his father-in-law, whose ancestors had been operating the Isle La Motte-Alburg ferry since 1805, out of business by building the first bridge between the towns. As a boy Goodsell sailed with his father in a schooner carrying stone from the Isle La Motte quarries for an addition to the Burlington breakwater. From then on, for seventy years, he never left the lake except for an interval as Collector of Customs at Alburg. His first ferries ran from Swanton to East Alburg and to Alburg Springs, from Windmill Point and Alburg to Rouses Point and from Grand Isle to Cumberland Head. No one ever knew where Captain Goodsell was going to turn up next, or with what kind of boat. He was cheerful, ingenious and utterly resilient to adversity, even if one of his ferries was at the bottom of the lake, which was the case more than once.

When the government threatened to tie up his 85-foot, double-ended steamer *Venus* because he was not complying with regulations for vessels over 65 feet in length, Goodsell beached the boat, sawed ten feet off both ends, planked them up and returned her to duty as a 65-footer, thus escaping the red tape for longer vessels. Once when the *Venus* was coming jauntily into the slip at Alburg and Goodsell's brother, Captain Bert, rang for full astern, the engineer, Julius Paquette, hollered up to the pilothouse: "Gee, Cap, we've lost our propellor!" Captain Bert emerged calmly from the pilothouse, walked to the bow and waved back the people standing on the dock. "Back up!" he told them. "We're coming right in here!" Come in they did, with a splintering crash. This accident and a congenital tendency to vibrate opened the seams of the *Venus* so that some nights rising water in the hull put out the banked fire in the boiler. Goodsell installed a gasoline pump to bail her out enough each morning so the boiler could be fired up. The steam pump took care of the leaks for the rest of the day.

One of Goodsell's more curious entries so far as propulsion was concerned was the *Dean Goodsell*, a steam cable barge which wound itself back and forth between Alburg and Rouses Point just a few yards south of the Canadian border. The cable ran 6,000 feet from shore to shore and in the middle of the channel rested on the bottom so as not to interfere with navigation. Securely fastened on both sides of the lake the cable passed through the hull of the sixteen-car barge and around a large drum. When the engine (which Elisha had salvaged from the *Venus*) was started, the drum gripped the cable and the barge forged ahead.

Among Goodsell's other island ferries was *The Twins* (purchased secondhand for the Alburg Center to Swanton run) which was steered by a sweep and whose fussy internal combustion engine was started with gas, then switched over to kerosene; and the *Sport*, an elegant 84-foot duplicate of the large lake steamers with paddle wheels and walking beam in miniature. Built in Newburgh, New York in 1881 as a private yacht she spent her twilight years paddling daintily back and forth south of the railroad bridge between Alburg and Rouses Point.

With two elderly ocean-going steam yachts, the *Admiral* and *Legonia H.*, plying between Burlington and Port Douglas (only a short distance south of Port Kent), Goodsell succeeded during the Twenties in cutting heavily into the traffic of the Transportation Company's large steamers. He advertised the lowest rates, the fastest service and the best boats, calmly surmounting every obstacle, including the sinking of the *Admiral* one night at her Burlington pier. When her fireman arrived early in the morning and saw only her stack and pilothouse above water he excitedly phoned Captain Goodsell, who showed no concern whatever and returned to bed. Later he was seen chuckling and swinging his arms as he strode down College Street toward the pier. "What did you think," he called to the fireman, "that we could raise her before breakfast?"

THE *Admiral*—BURLINGTON-PORT DOUGLAS FERRY SUNK AT HER DOCK
IN BURLINGTON.
Courtesy Special Collections, University of Vermont Library

N 1932 HE BOUGHT AT PUBLIC AUCTION THE PALATIAL TWO-DECK, 205-FOOT *Oneida*, originally the million-and-a-quarter-dollar yacht of William Randolph Hearst. A veteran of two trips to the Mediterranean and three to South America, the *Oneida* had oil-burning steam engines with a cruising radius of 4,000 miles. The fourteen men who looked after her polished engine and boiler rooms when she was a yacht were required to change their shoes three times enroute from boiler room to top deck. So silent was she underway that all that could be heard, even in the engine room, was the hiss of steam.

She had two galleys and a Gar Wood tender capable of sixty miles an hour, but what made her the talk of the oceans, not to mention Lake Champlain, were her princely staterooms. Colonel Lindbergh and Jack Dempsey lounged in them; Charlie Chaplin and Jimmy Walker; Pola Negri, Norma Talmadge and Greta Garbo. Marion Davies' suite had a gold bed and a carpet an inch and a half thick. The bathroom fixtures were of gold. The shower was entered through a glass door with a gold knob. Goodsell made the most of Miss Davies' quarters by levying an extra fee for admission. Beginning as it did in the pit of the Depression in 1932 the *Oneida's* career on Lake Champlain was brief. Partly scrapped in Burlington, her hull was later sold to a junk dealer and towed to St. Jean, Quebec.

This was somewhat the plight of the Transportation Company during the Roaring Twenties, for it was surrounded by competitors. Elisha Goodsell was syphoning off business to the north with his Island ferries and he was entrenched on the Burlington-Port Douglas run. The old company had never owned, nor seemingly cared to own, the Charlotte-Essex crossing nor those at Chimney, Larrabee or Chipman points, but they were all carrying cars now, and a car that crossed to the south did not cross from Burlington to Port Kent on the Transportation Company steamers. At Chipman Point was a cable ferry. Between Orwell and Montcalm Landing plied the odd *Ti-Orwell*, a paddleboat bearing an assortment of little buildings, as if a farmyard had been nailed to the deck. She had no smokestack and there was no other visible proof of a power plant. The paddles were turned by a heavy gasoline engine through a double-acting, two-way clutch and a cross-drive. The exhaust went overboard under the wheelhouse.

[Up north] for at least 84 years, until the Rouses Point automobile bridge opened in 1936, ferries ran from Isle LaMotte to Chazy, the earliest of them a scow with a sweep and sails. Franklin Hill, one of the proprietors, a stern, unyielding autocrat who lived to be 90 and wore the same hat for six decades, nevertheless accommodated local ladies by towing their rugs back and forth across the lake until they were clean.

20

LAUNCHED IN 1905, WILLIAM SWEET'S *The Twins* WAS THE FIRST
MOTORIZED FERRYBOAT ON LAKE CHAMPLAIN. IT WAS NAMED AFTER HIS
ONE-YEAR-OLD TWIN SONS, GERALD AND CLINTON.
Courtesy Gerald Sweet

The Twin Boys
Courtesy Special Collections, University of Vermont.

William Sweet, the last owner of the Chazy and Rouses Point ferries, in 1905 built a 60-foot-by-14-foot gasoline-powered vessel named *The Twins* (after his sons) to carry an already considerable cargo of automobiles. In 1916 *The Twins* was supplanted by a similar but more powerful fifteen-car ferry named *The Twin Boys* boasting, of all innovations, four lee boards which so impressed government inspectors that ferrymen from as far away as the Mississippi River used this vessel as a prototype. With the lee boards down at each landing, according to one inspector, "She's like a cow with four legs stuck in the mud—you can't move her."

Among the celebrities who crossed William Sweet's decks were Thomas Edison, Harvey Firestone, and Henry Ford on their camping trips.

From Chimney Point to Port Henry ran for decades the *G.R. Sherman*, a double-ended propellor steamer with a pepper-box pilothouse. The Captain's name was Weatherwax. Israel Kingdollar, engineer and first mate, always wore an old red flannel undershirt. The day in 1929 that they cut the ribbon opening traffic on the new bridge to Crown Point was, for Weatherwax and Kingdollar, Doomsday. When steelworkers jeered from the bridge, cruelly tossing bolts and nuts onto the deck of the *Sherman*, Weatherwax, his moustache bristling, shouted: "We'll run if we run for 25 cents!" Alas, clinkers replaced the glowing coals in the *Sherman's* boilers and she drifted off into oblivion. This was also the fate of the *Hildegarde*, originally a Vanderbilt racing sloop, which crossed from Arnold's Bay to Westport a few miles north.

ROM THE INLAND PORT OF VERGENNES SEVEN MILES UP THE OTTER, THE SMALL STEAMERS *Victor* and *Alexander* (replacing the *Water Lily* and *Little Nelly*) had for years maintained Captain Louis Daniels and his wife Philemon in comfortable circumstances. Philemon was the first woman in the world to carry a pilot's and master's license for a steamboat. With a boiler-room voice that belied her jingling chains and bracelets and rustling taffeta skirts, she wore her distinction well. When her husband died she steered the boats and collected the fares herself. Automobiles usually revived traffic on ferries fitted to carry them but they eventually put Philemon out of business since her steamers carried passengers only. At the turn of the century larger boats like the *A. Williams*, *Maquam* and *Reindeer* used to call at Vergennes although they had difficulty warping around one bend in the river. Captain Joy of the *Reindeer* was appropriately named. His tuneless whistle could be heard even on the foggy morning he planted his 180-foot boat in a mud bank.

STEAMER *Reindeer* — BUILT 1882 — THE ONLY STEAM BOAT ON LAKE
CHAMPLAIN THAT WAS NEVER PROPERTY OF C.T.Co.
Courtesy Special Collections, University of Vermont Library

By 1927 the *Charlotte-Essex* must have had more water behind her than any ferry in the world, for she was built in Athens, New York in 1869. Her vertical-beam engine was then secondhand since it had first served in the Hudson River ferry *J. T. Waterman*, built in 1858. The beam engine, one of the earliest, and, as refined for lake, sound and river paddleboats, the most reliable of all steam power plants, was simplicity itself. Its most prominent feature was its walking beam, one end of which was connected to the piston and the other to a long connecting rod which drove the paddles by way of a crank. The finest of these hand-built engines, gleaming with brass and polished steel, were made by Andrew Fletcher, a Scotsman whose shops were in Hoboken, New Jersey and whose handiwork was to be found in all of the later Champlain and Lake George sidewheelers.

Charlotte-Essex — Built in Athens, New York in 1869, she ran the
Charlotte-Essex crossing from 1921 to 1927.
Courtesy Captain Merritt Carpenter

Although the engine of the *Charlotte-Essex*, Fletcher's fourth, had by 1927 been running for 69 years it was still in good condition, although the wooden hull in which it served had become, as they say, a little peaked. As the *George H. Power*, the 12-car (or carriage) ferry had plied from Athens to Hudson, New York from 1869 to 1921. It was then brought up through the Champlain Canal for its six-year stint between Charlotte and Essex. During the last few seasons it was nip and tuck for Engineer Ralph Bigelow. The boiler inspectors had cut steam pressure from 40 to 25 pounds. On a rough day the hull had a sickening tendency to bend over the waves like a lily pad, opening the top of the slide ways, narrowing them at the bottom and cramping the engine's crosshead. Eventually the *Charlotte-Essex* migrated through the Chambly Canal to the St. Lawrence where she did not have to contend with waves and apparently ran several more years before she was at last called for by the old man with the scythe.

In 1926 25,000 cars crossed the lake on the five steamers then operating out of Burlington. The *Chateaugay*, *Ticonderoga* and *Vermont* of the Transportation Company ferried fifteen thousand to Port Kent and the rest crossed to Port Douglas on Goodsell's *Legonia* and *Admiral*. Four years later the C. T. Company was transporting 20,000 cars but since its paddleboats were large and expensive to operate and the *Vermont* was ploughing red ink on the north-south run to Montcalm Landing, the old company suspended all operations in 1932. The following year the Transportation Company turned the *Chateaugay* over to a group headed by Daniel Loomis, long the general manager. Operating as the Burlington-Port Kent ferry, this group also returned the *Ticonderoga* to service in 1936.

STEAMER A. *Williams*, 1870

New competition, however, was afoot in the person of Horace W. Corbin. Having won and lost a fortune in Mexican lumber Corbin was no stranger to finance, politics or the boating business, since his uncle had built the *A. Williams* for service between St. Albans and Plattsburgh. Corbin embellished his lakeside home on Grand Isle with mementoes of his ancestor, General Custer, with goldfish tanks set in the walls, and the yard outside with strutting peacocks, a jackass and other assorted animals. In a series of daring moves, reminiscent of the empire builders of the 19th century, Corbin obtained control of the Grand Isle to Cumberland Head ferry. In Burlington, flying the banner of the Green Mountain-Adirondack Ferry Company he laid down the keels of two large steel ferries, the *City of Burlington* and the *City of Plattsburgh*. He next bought the tottering Champlain Transportation Company, boats, docks, shipyard and charter. He tore the superstructure off the fifty-year old *Chateaugay*, sold her engines for scrap, cut the hull into sandwiches of steel and shipped them to Lake Winnepesaukee, where they were welded together to become the present motorship *Mount Washington III*. Scrapping all but the hull of the 262-foot *Vermont III* he redesigned her as an Atlantic coast diesel freighter. She long served in this capacity. With the advent of World War II he leased the Shelburne Shipyard to a firm making P.T. boats for the Navy. Faced with the spectre of gasoline rationing and the eclipse of the ferry business he sold at a great profit both the *City of Plattsburgh* and the *City of Burlington* to Electric Ferries, Inc. of New York, and the Gloucester-Yorktown Ferry Co. of Virginia, respectively. Since coal was not in short supply he put the *Ticonderoga* on extended ferry service between Burlington, Essex, Port Kent, Plattsburgh and Grand Isle to transport the thousands of people who could not drive their cars.

City of Burlington AND *City of Plattsburgh*—STREAMLINE FERRIES BUILT
IN BURLINGTON BY HORACE CORBIN IN 1936 AND 1937 RESPECTIVELY,
FOR BURLINGTON-PORT KENT FERRY SERVICE

Corbin was meanwhile playing a game of financial roulette during which he almost lost the Transportation Company to a group of bankers from Plattsburgh and Ausable Forks. Having loaned Corbin a large sum the New Yorkers obviously were maneuvering in 1939-40 to gain control of the company, but their plans were scotched by the actions of a Vermont lawyer and stockholder, an associate of Corbin's, who sought redress in the federal district court of the free-styled Vermont judge, Harland B. Howe. Excoriating the New York bankers for unethical practices in a manner that Ethan Allen would have found satisfying, Judge Howe is reported to have exclaimed in one hearing: "You New Yorkers aren't satisfied to milk the cow, you want to strip her!" At length two Burlington banks stepped in and removed the company's encumbrances across the lake.

The Corbin era ended in 1948 when Lewis P. Evans, Jr., Richard H. Wadhams and James G. Wolcott, a triumverate grounded in corporate management, engineering and finance bought the old company and set to work acquiring and building steel ferries for their three crossings, now including that from Charlotte to Essex. For a few years prior to the purchase of this crossing by the Transportation Company, Captain Wally Mock, who sailed the last of the lake's freight-carrying sloops, operated the diesel ferry *Plattsburgh* there. He had brought her from the overcrowded Grand Isle-Cumberland Head crossing and remodeled her pilothouse so that

Plattsburgh WAS BUILT IN WHITEHALL, NEW YORK IN 1923.
SHOWN HERE IN 1933 OFF ESSEX, NEW YORK.
Courtesy Alice Mock Tart

it was only five feet two inches high, exactly fitting Wally. If he had something better to do, like tuning up the engine of his car or changing a flat tire, ferry passengers waited. While standing on the dock at Burlington one day in a big blow from the north, Wally watched one of the ferries rolling and pitching toward the gap in the breakwater. "Got a pretty bottom, ain't she!" he said. A kind of grim humor dominated the struggles of the first years as the new owners of the Transportation Company strove to advance simultaneously on all fronts. As some cribbing from their Burlington dock floated past the office window one spring during high water President Evans remarked: "The trouble with wood is that it rots." Shortly thereafter the derrick boat sank, causing further deferment of deferred maintenance. And the aging Grand Isle-Cumberland Head ferry *Roosevelt II* almost sank in 1952 when a wave forced her against submerged piling in Burlington. Seven years later they towed her out into the broad lake and the president of the company himself chopped several holes in her hull. But this time, true to her Vermont heritage, the *Roosevelt II* was not inclined to sink. With several more holes, she was dispatched at last.

THE WOODEN HULLED *Roosevelt II* RAN BETWEEN GRAND ISLE,
VERMONT AND CUMBERLAND HEAD, NEW YORK. SHE WAS 36 YEARS
OLD WHEN SHE WAS DELIBERATELY SUNK IN THE BROAD LAKE IN 1959.

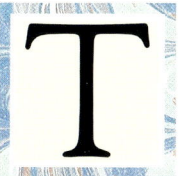HERE ARE NO WOODEN HULLS SERVING ANY OF THE THREE ROUTES TODAY. MANY DECADES have passed since Sam Rice of Cold Springs bent against his 14-foot oars and rowed his last load of passengers to Dresden. Where wind, horses and steam once reigned from Charlotte to Essex a small diesel single-ender brought up from New York the steel *Juniper*, throbbed for fifteen years. She was originally owned by the Pepsi-Cola Company and named the *Big Bottle*—what else? She was succeeded by the 65-foot *Essex*, then the 80-foot *Abnaki*, then the 100-foot *Mt. Mansfield*, all built by Blount Marine of Rhode Island especially for service on Lake Champlain. In 1971 a new keel was laid there for the 100-foot *Mt. Marcy*, named for the highest Adirondack peak, to complement her sister ship, named for Vermont's highest Green Mountain.

Burlington to Port Kent is today a three-ferry route consisting of the 50-car, 190-foot *Valcour*, built at Shelburne Harbor in 1947, and the two-deckers *Adirondack* and *Champlain*. Whereas the lake's first modern steel ferries migrated south, the *Adirondack* and *Champlain*, formerly the *Governor Emerson C. Harrington* and *City of Hampton*, respectively, were built down country and came north. The *Mott Haven* arrived on Lake Champlain in 1945 from New York, where she had served on the Riker's Island run, only to be sold to Huntington Hartford in 1961 and to depart for Nassau in the Bahamas.

To the odyssey of migrating ferries must be added the *Essex* which on February 8, 1970 reached Puerto Matios de Galves, Guatemala by way of the Champlain Canal, Hudson River, and the Sound to Rhode Island for fitting out; then along the coast to Chesapeake Bay, southward from Norfolk, Virginia to Southport, North Carolina via the Intra Coastal Waterway, by ocean to Florida, again by the Waterway from Cape Canaveral to the St. Lucie River, across Lake Okeechobee and down the Caloosahatchee River to Fort Myers on Florida's west coast, and seaward to the Gulf of Mexico and the Yucatan Channel. Stiff winds, sometimes reducing to a standstill what veteran Captain Robert L. Hempstead called his "sixty-five-foot pumpkin seed," yielded to the dominantly easterly trades south of Cape Antonio and fine sailing to the Gulf of Honduras.

H EMPSTEAD'S EVEN MORE EPIC DELIVERY OF THE *Abnaki* TO KETCHIKAN, ALASKA BY WAY OF the Panama Canal and the entire North American coast consumed 7,600 miles, many of them, even around Cape Hatteras, by "log, lead, and lookout" (the radar equipment defied every attempt at repairs from Rhode Island to California).

The [one] ferry at the southern end of the lake is still independent. A tug lashed alongside, it crosses from Larrabee's Point to Ticonderoga. The only vestige of the old days is the last of the paddleboats, *Ticonderoga*, which completed 43 seasons of operation in 1953 and two years later was transported nearly two miles overland to the grounds of the Shelburne Museum where she was restored to pristine condition.

Perhaps a steam whistle, piped to a boiler powered by atomic fission, will again be heard blowing for a landing a century from now. Maybe tomorrow's generations will skim over the waves in hydrofoil boats. But pass the broad lake in ships they must, until the lake runs dry.

THE *Juniper* RAN 15 YEARS AT THE CHARLOTTE-ESSEX CROSSING.
SHE OPERATES CURRENTLY AS A CRUISE & DINNER BOAT OUT OF
PLATTSBURGH, NEW YORK.

City of Hampton WITH HER SUPERSTRUCTURE LOWERED FOR HER PASSAGE
NORTH THROUGH THE CHAMPLAIN CANAL.
SHE WAS REASSEMBLED IN VERMONT AND RENAMED *Champlain*.

26

VERMONT BUILT *Valcour* OF THE BURLINGTON-PORT KENT CROSSING.
CIRCA 1952

Adirondack AT THE BEGINNING OF HER CAREER ON LAKE CHAMPLAIN-
LANDING AT PORT KENT, NEW YORK-CIRCA 1956

Abnaki—BUILT FOR THE CHARLOTTE-ESSEX CROSSING IN 1967,
THE 80' *Abnaki* SAILED FOR KETCHIKAN, ALASKA IN 1970
Photo Courtesy Clyde Smith

T HE RECENT HISTORY OF LAKE CHAMPLAIN FERRYBOATS, WITH THE EXCEPTION OF THE FORT Ticonderoga ferry, is, by and large, the history of the boats of the Lake Champlain Transportation Company. Following is a chronology of this company's ferryboat developments since Ralph Nading Hill's story brought us up to 1972. (by Jerry P. Williams, Bird J. Bombard, William Wolcott, Roxanne Wolcott, Bill Pinney, and Brian Cudahy)

In May 1974, the *Algonquin*, a sister to the *Abnaki*, was also sold to the State of Alaska. She served as a relief to the *Abnaki*, ferrying passengers and vehicles between the mainland and Ketchikan International Airport on Gravina Island.

Back on Lake Champlain, growth at the 1.9 mile Grand Isle-Cumberland Head crossing warranted building a larger vessel for that run. In the spring of 1975 the 30-car, 142-foot, two-engined *Governor Aiken* was built by Blount Marine of Warren, Rhode Island to replace the overburdened *Mt. Mansfield*.

THE *Governor Aiken* RUNS BETWEEN CHARLOTTE, VERMONT
AND ESSEX, NEW YORK

In August of 1975, while tacking in a rough sea, the 190-foot *Valcour* of the Burlington-Port Kent line grounded on Ferris Reef off Port Kent, New York. The passengers were quickly removed by the *Governor Aiken*, dispatched immediately from her run at Grand Isle. Within a day the *Valcour's* full load of vehicles had been unloaded onto the *Governor Aiken* and the *Mt. Marcy*. Two days later, after an on-the-spot attempt at patching her damaged hull had failed, and with a rising sea threatening to lift her off the reef that was keeping her afloat, the *Valcour* was dragged off with the aid of a tug. With her bow awash, the anxious crew backed the vessel to the nearest beach at Port Kent, New York, almost two miles away. Now safely grounded, the vessel was fitted with a temporary patch, the flooded compartments were pumped, and the boat made her way to the Shelburne Shipyard in Vermont for permanent repairs. Later, a decision was made to dismantle the rudders and propellors from the bow and run the boat single-ended; that is, unlike the rest of the fleet, she would be propelled from one end only. The hope was that the vessel would be faster, use less fuel, and require less maintenance. This proved to be the case, and the *Valcour* continues to operate this way.

In 1976, Ray Pecor Jr. of Shelburne, Vermont bought the Lake Champlain Transportation Company from Lewis P. Evans, Jr., Richard H. Wadhams, and James G. Wolcott. One of Mr. Pecor's first opportunities to experience the vagaries of owning a ferry company came that spring with an unusually high lake level that damaged shoreside ferry property. Access to their offices flooded so badly the staff of the ferry company had to row or wade to work until the water receded. Ray Pecor was undaunted though, for that year, in spite of many unknowns, he decided to take a risk that could have a big reward, both for ferry commuters and for the ferry company. He decided to attempt to run a ferry through the winter ice on the busy Grand Isle-Cumberland Head ferry crossing. Due to lake ice, the ferry had been forced to tie-up an average of eighty-two days each winter. Needless to say, this was a significant inconvenience to most commuters. They were now forced to drive the extra fifty miles in winter conditions via the Rouses Point bridge farther north. Some commuters were reluctant to acknowledge a problem even existed. They simply looked at the ice across the lake as a temporary bridge. They established their own temporary "highway" across the ice just north of

Grand Isle — THE FIRST VESSEL TO RUN YEAR-ROUND ON LAKE CHAMPLAIN

the ferry route. Snow whiteouts, fog, and spring thaws added an element of excitement to this method; too much of an element for most travelers.

In 1977, in one of the coldest winters on record, the 132-foot ferry *Grand Isle* succeeded in running continuously through the winter ice, a milestone in Lake Champlain ferry history. One difficulty arose when the vessel froze into its slip on particularly cold and windless nights. The crews hoped for heavy trucks on their first trip. The weight of a heavy vehicle, settling the boat, broke the grasp of the ice just enough to let the boat's power finish the job. Another problem resulted when ice floes drifted in under the loading ramps, became compacted, and impeded the ramps' operation. A bubbling system was subsequently designed that was instrumental in keeping the ferry from freezing in overnight. A flushing system was also designed to prevent ice from collecting under the ramps.

The winter ferry operation proved a major commercial success. Having a reliable year-round ferry crossing was a real boon to travelers and to commerce in the upstate Vermont and New York areas.

I N 1978 THE WRECK OF THE *Phoenix* WAS DISCOVERED BY DIVERS NEAR COLCHESTER SHOAL, north of Burlington. The *Phoenix* was built at Vergennes, Vermont in 1815 and was the second steamboat to operate on the lake. On the night of September 5, 1819, under the command of Captain Richard Sherman, the *Phoenix* caught fire while crossing from Burlington to Port Kent and six passengers lost their lives. She burned to the waterline and fetched up on the Shoals of Colchester. Later, the winter ice carried the hull underwater onto the steep face of the shoal.

Today, the *Phoenix* rests with its bow in 60 and its stern in 110 feet of water, the oldest known steamboat hull in the world. An archaeological investigation of the wreck has yielded much new information about the construction of early steamboats. It was determined she was very strongly built, and in contrast to her boxy predecessor, the *Vermont*, had a rounded hull. The *Phoenix* has recently been designated by the State of Vermont an "Underwater Historic Preserve," an innovative program which encourages divers to safely and responsibly view her underwater. The *Phoenix* and other shipwrecks of Lake Champlain are a valuable legacy of the lake's proud historic past.

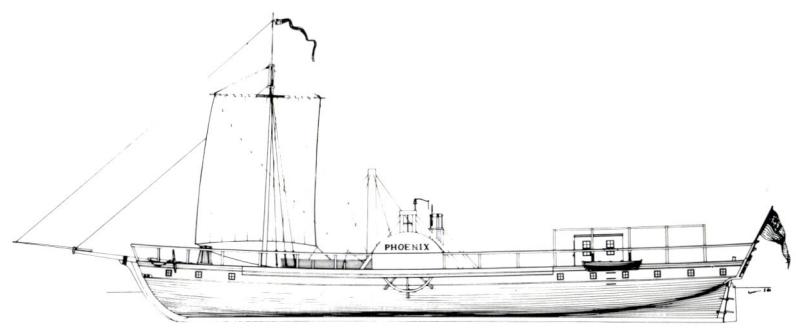

LAKE CHAMPLAIN STEAMBOAT COMPANY STEAMER *Phoenix* WHICH PLIED
THE LAKE FOR FOUR YEARS UNTIL DESTROYED BY FIRE IN 1818. THE
DRAWING IS BASED ON ARCHAEOLOGICAL MEASUREMENTS OF THE HULL
AND CONTEMPORARY PLANS OF SIMILAR STEAMERS. DRAWING BY KEVIN CRISMAN.
Courtesy Vermont Division for Historic Preservation

On September 12, 1979, a weather condition foreign to Vermont led the Lake Champlain Transportation Company to dispatch the Charlotte ferry *Mt. Marcy* to Mobile, Alabama. Hurricane Frederic had destroyed the causeway connecting the community of Dauphin Island to mainland Alabama. Until that causeway was replaced, people and supplies had to be ferried to the island by water. On February 14, 1980, the *Mt. Marcy* began service between makeshift docks on Dauphin Island and mainland Alabama. She was joined later by the *Mt. Mansfield*. For more than two years, they were the primary link in ferrying construction supplies to a badly damaged island. Both boats ran the sixteen-mile crossing until a bridge replacing the causeway opened in 1982. It was a peculiar sight; two ferries from Burlington, Vermont, named after Vermont and New York's highest peaks—Mt. Mansfield and Mt. Marcy—both crewed with skippers from Vermont, now running in the Deep South. Where they had sailed in fresh, deep water cradled by the Adirondack and Green Mountains, they now plied the shallow, brackish waters of Mobile Bay.

In August of 1981, the 20-car, 100-foot, single ended ferry *Essex* was built for the Lake Champlain Transportation Company, again by the Blount Marine Company. With the *Mt Marcy* and the *Mt. Mansfield* now busy in Mobile Bay, the *Essex* was needed to assist in handling traffic on the Charlotte-Essex ferry crossing.

Essex WITH A FULL LOAD ON THE CHARLOTTE, VERMONT-ESSEX, NEW YORK CROSSING

EWFOUNDLAND, CANADA WAS THE NEXT LOCALE TO MAKE USE OF THE LAKE CHAMPLAIN Transportation Company fleet. From September of 1984 to May of 1985, the Newfoundland government needed a fill-in vessel to ferry passengers, vehicles, and supplies between Pilley's Island and Long Island, on the northern coast of Newfoundland. The Lake Champlain ferry *Charlotte* and her two Vermont skippers were signed on for the job. The 91-foot ferry *Charlotte*, formerly the Chesapeake Bay marine research vessel *Langley*, had been purchased by the ferry company in 1980 and sailed to Lake Champlain late that year for conversion to an auto ferry. In the spring of 1981, the conversion complete, the *Charlotte* was christened as a car ferry. She ran the Charlotte-Essex ferry crossing until she was called for in Newfoundland. On her way north, at St. John's, Newfoundland, ramps were attached at each end so the *Charlotte* could handle vehicles in the slips at the islands.

The *Charlotte* was subsequently sent directly to Mobile, Alabama. Although the *Mt. Marcy* had returned to Vermont shortly after the Dauphin Island causeway had reopened, the *Mt. Mansfield* had been "testing the waters" on a new ferry crossing in Mobile Bay. This route connected Dauphin Island with Fort Morgan at Gulf Shores, three miles to the west. The route eliminated a lengthy journey for travelers seeking a direct coastal route along the Alabama shore. The crossing proved so popular that the *Charlotte* joined the run and within a year the decision was made to lengthen her by cutting her in half and adding a midsection. She was also widened and repowered.

Back on Lake Champlain, thanks in large part to the year-round operation, business was growing at the Grand Isle crossing, making it evident that soon two-boat winter service would be necessary. The *Governor Aiken* was able to run through the winters of 1982 and 1983, but her success these two winters was tenuous. She did not have the power of the *Grand Isle* to push through the ice nor was she built as strongly. The *Governor Aiken's* ability to stick to a winter schedule, therefore, depended on the cooperation of the winter weather; this was hard to count on. So the Lake Champlain Transportation Company built a ferry that could operate dependably in the winter conditions and handle the traffic growth. Eastern Marine of Panama City, Florida won the contract and laid the keel for the 172-foot, two-engined ferry. This boat was equipped with stainless steel propellors, one at each end. They were much more resistant to ice damage than the more traditional bronze propellors. Each end of the double-ended ferry was reinforced, giving it the strength to shoulder through the heavy ice floes encountered on the winter crossing. Named the *Plattsburgh* the 40-car vessel was on the run in late 1984, ensuring reliable, year-round, two-boat service on the Grand Isle crossing.

Plattsburgh IN EARLY MORNING SUN AT THE GRAND ISLE FERRY CROSSING

In the spring of 1987 the *Mt. Marcy*, again under the command of Captain Hempstead, was sold to the state of Alaska to assist, as did her predecessors, in the moving of traffic between the mainland and Ketchikan International Airport on Gravina Island. This time she left her old home on the Charlotte-Essex crossing for good. The *Governor Aiken*, no longer needed in Grand Isle, was sent south to Charlotte to replace the *Mt. Marcy*.

Evans-Wadhams-Wolcott RUNNING IN WINTER ICE AT THE YEAR-ROUND
GRAND ISLE-CUMBERLAND HEAD FERRY CROSSING

By 1988, increased traffic at the Grand Isle ferry crossing mandated another addition to the Lake Champlain Transportation Company fleet. The 188-foot, 45-car *Evans-Wadhams-Wolcott*, named after the previous owners of the Lake Champlain Transportation Company, was built by Houma Fabricators of Houma, Louisiana and was on the run at Grand Isle by late spring of that year. She also was equipped and built for winter operation.

1988 was an important year for the Lake Champlain Transportation Company for another, more nostalgic reason. The *Adirondack*, the oldest vessel in the fleet, was commemorated on her seventy-fifth anniversary. She began her career as the *South Jacksonville* in 1913, operating in Florida on the St. John's River between downtown Jacksonville and South Jacksonville. A bridge put an end to that run in 1921. She served next on the Delaware River as the *Mount Holly*, owned by the Tacony-Palmyra Ferry Company. In 1927, the *Mount Holly* went into service in New York City on the East River between Long Island City and the foot of East 34th Street. She was owned by the 34th Street Vehicular Ferry Company. The company failed and the Great Depression, along with the increased construction of bridges and tunnels, made the future of the *Mount Holly* look somewhat dismal. But in 1938 the Chesapeake Bay Ferry Company purchased her. At this point her superstructure underwent a major rebuilding giving her, essentially, the appearance she has today. Her name was changed to the *Governor Emerson C. Harrington 2nd*. She ran on Eastern Bay on the Chesapeake Bay connecting the communities of Clairborne and Romancoke. In 1945 her original coal-fired steam engine was removed and replaced with two six-cylinder Atlas Imperial diesel engines. But when the first span of the Chesapeake Bay Bridge opened in 1952, the State of Maryland ceased its ferryboat operations and the *Governor Emerson C. Harrington 2nd* was for sale.

The Lake Champlain Transportation Company purchased the ferry in 1954, and renamed her the *Adirondack* after the mountain range in upper New York State. So that she would fit under the low bridge clearance (13 ft.) of the Champlain Canal, her upper deck was lowered to the car deck for the passage.

Except for some brief stints on the Charlotte-Essex ferry crossing, the *Adirondack* has sailed every summer between Burlington, Vermont and Port Kent, New York since 1954. Her only major modification since then was the replacement of her Atlas Imperial diesel engines with two 12V71 Detroit Diesel engines in 1970.

The *Adirondack* is currently the oldest double-ended ferryboat under United States registry. If the *Adirondack* is an officially enrolled United States merchant vessel on November 23, 1992, she will replace the Hudson River ferryboat *Lackawanna* as the oldest, in-service, double-ended ferryboat of all time.

Adirondack (BUILT IN 1913)—RUNS BETWEEN BURLINGTON, VERMONT
AND PORT KENT, NEW YORK—NEW YORK'S ADIRONDACK MOUNTAINS
ARE IN BACKGROUND

ADIRONDACK

Roll Call of Early Lake Champlain Vessels

Sailing Ships Built Prior to 1815				Sidewheel Steamers on Lake Champlain			

Name	Tons	Yr. Built	Where Built	Name	Yr. Built	Where Built	Lgth
Unknown	30	1790	Burlington	Vermont	1808	Burlington	120
Dolphin	30	1793	Burlington	Phoenix	1815	Vergennes	146
Burlington Packet	30	1793	Burlington	Champlain	1816	Vergennes	90
Maria	30	1795	Burlington	Congress	1818	Vergennes	108
Lady Washington	30	1795	Burlington	Phoenix II	1820	Vergennes	150
Burlington Packet	30	1796	Burlington	Gen. Greene	1825	Shelburne	75
Unknown	30	1800	Burlington	Franklin	1827	St. Albans	162
Union	30	1800	Burlington	Washington	1827	Essex	92
Elizabeth	40	1800	Essex	McDonough	1828	St. Albans	89
Jupiter	40	1802	Essex	Winooski	1832	Shelburne	136
Juno	40	1802	Essex	Water Witch	1832	Fort Cassin, Vt.	90
Unetta	30	1803	Essex	Burlington	1837	Shelburne	190
Independence	35	1805	Essex	Whitehall	1838	Whitehall	215
Privateer	40	1807	Burlington	Saranac	1842	Shelburne	166
Hunter	50	1809	Burlington	Francis Saltus	1844	Whitehall	185
Emperor	50	1810	Barber's Point	United States	1847	Shelburne	240
Rising Sun	50	1810	Essex	Boston	1851	Shelburne	127
Eagle	60	1810	Whitehall	America	1851	Whitehall	250
Essex	50	1810	Essex	Canada	1853	Whitehall	260
Boston	30	1810	Burlington	Montreal	1856	Shelburne	224
Saucy Fox	50	1810	Essex	Adirondack	1867	Shelburne	251
Gold Hunter	50	1811	Whitehall	Oakes Ames (later Champlain)	1868	Marks Bay (Burlington)	258
President	75	1812	Essex	A. Williams	1870	Marks Bay	132
Fair Trader	75	1812	Essex	Vermont II	1871	Shelburne	272
Morning Star	50	1812	Whitehall	Maquam	1880	Swanton	142
Jacob Bunker	65	1812	Burlington	Reindeer	1881	Alburg	180
Richard	60	1813	Essex	Chateaugay	1887	Shelburne	205
Leopard	50	1813	Essex	Vermont III	1903	Shelburne	262
Boxer	50	1813	Essex	Ticonderoga	1906	Shelburne	220
Paragon	75	1814	Burlington				

(Many of the above paddle boats operated also as ferries
during their long service as line boats)

Principal Ferries on Lake Champlain Since World War I

Name	Off. No.	Where Built	Type	Length	Route
Abnaki	509538	Warren, R.I., 1967	Diesel screw	80	Charlotte-Essex
Adirondack	211156	Jacksonville, Fla., 1913	Diesel screw	130	Burlington-Port Kent
Admiral	106921	Providence, R.I., 1892	Steam screw yacht	117.7	Burlington-Port Douglas
Alexander	107465	Vergennes, Vt., 1897	Steam screw	58	Vergennes-Westport
Algonquin	514755	Warren, R.I., 1968	Diesel screw	80	Grand Isle-Cumberland Head
Angia	218902	East Alburg, Vt., 1916	Gasoline screw	49	East Alburg-West Swanton
Champlain	169008	Cohoes, N.Y., 1922	Wood scow; aux. power	61	Larrabee's Point-Fort Ticonderoga
Champlain	229460	Baltimore, Md., 1930	Diesel screw	148.3	Burlington-Port Kent
Charlotte	D501445	Baltimore, Md., 1952	Diesel screw	112.6	Charlotte-Essex
Charlotte-Essex	85171	Athens, N.Y., 1869	Steam sidewheel	95	Charlotte-Essex
City of Burlington	235212	Burlington, Vt., 1936	Diesel screw	152	(a) Burlington-Port Douglas
					(b) Burlington-Port Kent
City of Plattsburgh	236530	Burlington, Vt., 1937	Diesel screw	152	Burlington-Port Kent
Cumberland	217495	Swanton, Vt., 1919	Steam screw	64.6	Grand Isle-Cumberland Head
Dean Goodsell	86463	Burlington, Vt., 1927	Steam cable barge	64	Alburg-Rouses Point
Essex	503775	Warren, R.I. 1966	Diesel screw	65	(a) Grand Isle-Cumberland Head
					(b) Charlotte-Essex
Essex	D639911	Warren, R.I. 1981	Diesel screw	100	Charlotte-Essex
Evans, Wadhams, Wolcott	D931211	Houma, LA, 1988	Diesel screw	188	Grand Isle-Cumberland Head
Fort Ticonderoga	253748	Daviesville, R.I., 1947	Cable barge; aux. towboat	75	Larrabee's Point-Fort Ticonderoga
Fort Ticonderoga II	278723	Warren, R.I., 1959	Cable barge; aux. towboat	106	Larrabee's Point-Fort Ticonderoga
G.R. Sherman	86463	Champlain, N.Y., 1890	Steam screw	75	Chimney Point-Port Henry
Governor George D. Aiken	D566265	Warren, R.I., 1975	Diesel screw	132	(a) Grand Isle-Cumberland Head
					(b) Charlotte-Essex
Grand Isle	266081	Tampa, Fla., 1953	Diesel screw	132.1	Grand Isle-Cumberland Head
Hildegarde	13005	Islip, N.Y., 1876	Steam screw	64	Arnold's Bay-Westport
Juniper	249023	Yonkers, N.Y., 1945	Diesel screw	62.3	Charlotte-Essex
Kittery	161161	Kennebunkport, Me.	Steam sidewheel	83.6	Grand Isle-Cumberland Head
Legonia II	206627	Wilmington, Del., 1909	Steam screw yacht	140.4	Burlington-Port Douglas
Mott Haven	227200	Brooklyn, N.Y.	Diesel screw	99.4	Burlington-Port Kent
Mt. Mansfield	521774	Warren, R.I., 1969	Diesel screw	100	(a) Grand Isle-Cumberland Head
					(b) Charlotte-Essex
Mt. Marcy	539779	Warren, R.I., 1971	Diesel screw	100	Charlotte-Essex
Oneida	......	Newburgh, N.Y.	Steam screw yacht	212	Burlington-Port Douglas
Plattsburgh	223013	Whitehall, N.Y., 1923	Diesel screw	79.7	(a) Grand Isle-Cumberland Head
					(b) Charlotte-Essex
Plattsburgh	D676440	Panama City, Fla. 1984	Diesel screw	172.5	Grand Isle-Cumberland Head
Roosevelt	203203	Milford, Del., 1906	Steam screw	114	Grand Isle-Cumberland Head
Roosevelt II	223266	Nyack, N.Y., 1923	Diesel screw	108	Grand Isle-Cumberland Head
Sport	115767	Newburgh, N.Y., 1881	Steam sidewheel	84	Windmill Point-Rouses Point
Stanley B	222430	Swanton, Vt., 1922	Gasoline cable	65	(a) East Alburg-Swanton
					(b) Chipman Point-Wrights
New Alburg Springs Ferry	218636	Alburg Springs, Vt., 1919	Gasoline screw	55.4	Alburg Springs-Swanton
The Twins	203310	Champlain, N.Y., 1905	Gasoline screw	60	(a) Isle LaMotte-Chazy
					(b) Alburg Center-Swanton
					(c) Windmill Point-Rouses Point
The Twin Boys	213955	Champlain, N.Y., 1916	Gasoline screw	....	Isle LaMotte-Chazy
Ticonderoga	169525	Whitehall, N.Y., 1924	Barge; auxiliary power	50	Orwell-Ticonderoga
Ti-Orwell (I & II)	210567 226371	Ticonderoga, N.Y. I 1916, II 1926	Gasoline sidewheel	49 57	Orwell-Ticonderoga
Valcour	253785	Shelburne, Vt., 1947	Diesel screw	190	Burlington-Port Kent
Venus	209930	Massena, N.Y.	Steam screw	85	Windmill Point-Rouses Point

Evans-Wadhams-Wolcott AND *Plattsburgh* IN ICE
AT GRAND ISLE FERRY CROSSING.